Grandmothers at Work

Meet My Grandmother

She's a United States Senator

★ ★ ★

By Lisa Tucker McElroy
(with help from Eileen
Feinstein Mariano)

Photographs by Joel Benjamin

THE MILLBROOK PRESS
BROOKFIELD, CONNECTICUT

This book is for Valerie Tucker and Veronica McElroy,

both teachers, both brand-new grandmothers.

ACKNOWLEDGMENTS

Rosalind Wyman; Trevor Daley, Debbie Mesloh, Bill Chandler, Samantha Smith, Jim Hock, and Julie Hansen in Senator Feinstein's office; the United States Senate; the White House; City Hall, San Francisco, California; Katherine Feinstein and Rick Mariano; Mark Gardner, photographic assistant; Senator Joseph Lieberman; Erika Giraldo-Martin; Kimber MacGibbon; Dr. Todd Shapiro and his office staff; Dr. Susan Bennett; the Tucker and McElroy families; Bob Dorsey; Elizabeth Terris; and, as always, my wonderful family, Stephen and Joe McElroy.

Photographs courtesy of Robert Dorsey: pp. 3, 6 (bottom); Liaison Agency: p. 12; The White House and Senator Feinstein's Office: pp. 13, 16; Morris & Carrick: p. 17 (top); © 1992 Kevin Horan: p. 17 (bottom); Senator Feinstein's Office: p. 18 (both); Elizabeth Terris: p. 30

Library of Congress Cataloging-in-Publication Data
McElroy, Lisa Tucker.
Meet my grandmother : she's a United States senator / by Lisa Tucker McElroy
(with help from Eileen Feinstein Mariano) ; photographs by Joel Benjamin.
p. cm – (Grandmothers at work)
Summary: Describes the busy life of Senator Dianne
Feinstein of California, seen through the eyes of her
six-year-old granddaughter.
ISBN 0-7613-1721-X (lib. bdg.)   0-7613-1432-6 (pbk.)
1. Feinstein, Dianne, 1933—Juvenile literature. 2. Women legislators—United States—Biography—Juvenile literature. 3. Legislators—United States—Biography—Juvenile literature. 4. United States. Congress. Senate—Biography—Juvenile literature. 5. Grandmothers—United States—Biography—Juvenile literature. 6. Granddaughters—United States—Biography—Juvenile literature. (1. Feinstein, Dianne, 1933- 2. Legislators. 3. Women—Biography. 4. Grandmothers. 5. Children's writings.)
I. Mariano, Eileen Feinstein. II. Benjamin, Joel, ill. III. Title. IV. Series.
E840.8.F45 M38 2000   328.73'092—dc21   (B)   99-046202

Published by The Millbrook Press, Inc.
2 Old New Milford Road, Brookfield, Connecticut 06804
www.millbrookpress.com

I love visiting

City Hall in San Francisco. A few months ago my kindergarten class went on a field trip there, and we saw a statue of a lady outside the Mayor's office. When my teacher asked if anyone knew who the lady was, I jumped up and down and raised my hand high and answered that it was my grandmother. My name is Eileen Feinstein Mariano, and I'm six years old. My grandmother, Dianne Feinstein, used to be the Mayor of San Francisco. Now she is a United States Senator.

★

This statue stands right outside the Mayor's office, where my grandmother used to work.

DIANNE FEINSTEIN

MEMBER
BOARD OF SUPERVISORS
1970 – 1978

PRESIDENT
BOARD OF SUPERVISORS

3

I call my grandmother Gagi, which rhymes with foggy. Her statue is in City Hall. But then she decided that she would like to help all the people of California, so she became a United States Senator. Now she mostly works in Washington, D.C.

★

This domed building is the U. S. Capitol, where the Senate meets. It is in the middle of Capitol Hill in Washington, D.C.

The Senators from the largest states have their offices in the Hart Senate Office Building. It is new and has lots of space.

Gagi has to work very hard when she is in Washington, D.C. In the morning she goes to her office in the **Hart Senate Office Building** on Capitol Hill.

5

Gagi usually starts her day with a cup of coffee and then has a meeting with some of her staffers. These are the people who help her do her work. She has forty staffers in this Washington office, so when everyone gets together, the room is pretty crowded!

Gagi tells the staffers what she wants to work on that day, and they tell her about any important changes in the law or in current events.

Staffers have to make sure that Gagi knows all about things that are important to Californians and to all Americans. Staffers also read all of Gagi's mail, which is a big job, because she gets about ten thousand letters every week. And you know what? She does her best to see that every single letter gets an answer.

Can you believe how many people write letters to Gagi?

After meeting with staffers,

Gagi sits in her office and does work on her computer and makes phone calls. I think she misses us, because she has a lot of pictures of our family on her desk. She also has pictures of flowers on her wall, which she drew herself! I like Snickers a lot and so does Gagi, so she has a big bowl of them near the couch across from her desk. The coolest things in her office are the TV that allows her to see what is happening on the Senate floor and a special clock that alerts her when votes are about to take place.

★

In the glass case behind Gagi, you can see lots of caps and other souvenirs from California.

Don't these flowers look real?

These constituents came to Gagi's office to talk to her about their jobs as carpenters in California.

One fun part of Gagi's job is meeting with

constituents when they visit Washington. *Constituent* is the official word for someone who lives in the state a Senator represents. So, since I'm from California, I'm one of Gagi's constituents. Constituents are always welcome to come to her office and say hello. After all, the only reason she is in Washington is because we elected her to go there and help us.

Gagi likes to answer letters in the morning and work on different bills that she wants help with from other Senators. A bill is a law that has not yet been passed by the Senate and the House of Representatives. Every year Gagi proposes about fifty bills, either by herself or with other Senators. Not all the bills become laws, but a lot do. Some of Gagi's most important bills are about education and crime and protecting our natural parks and forests.

As Gagi works on bills on her computer, she calls other Senators about them, and talks to constituents about what they would like the bills to say.

★

After they become laws, Gagi hangs framed copies of her favorite bills on the walls of her office.

9

When a bill is ready for the other Senators to vote on, Gagi gives a speech about it on the Senate floor in the Capitol building. To go from her office to the Capitol building, Gagi takes the elevator down to the basement. If she's in a big hurry, she can press a special button that only Senators are allowed to use. Then the elevator will come immediately! Gagi takes a special tram that runs between the Senate office buildings and the Capitol. It sure doesn't look like the cable car trams that we have in San Francisco, but I guess the idea is the same.

THIS ELEVATOR IS RESERVED FOR SENATORS ONLY AT ALL TIMES

★

I think it is pretty neat that there is a tram running below the ground on Capitol Hill, just like a real subway!

Sometimes Gagi

runs into other Senators on the tram, and they get a chance to talk about Senate business or just chat about their families. Lots of the other Senators are Gagi's friends.

★

Sometimes Gagi rides the tram with her friend Senator Joseph Lieberman, who represents the people of Connecticut.

11

It's funny that they call the big round room where the Senate meets the Senate floor. It's in the Capitol building, and all the Senators get together there to discuss which bills should become laws. When Gagi makes a speech, she stands at the front of the room, and the Senators sit at little desks and listen to her. The desks curve around the Senate floor in a half circle, so that all the Senators can see and hear whoever is speaking at the podium at the front. The Republicans sit on one side, and the Democrats sit on the other.

When Gagi or any other U.S. Senator meets with the president, he listens carefully to what the Senator says.

When a bill Gagi has written gets passed by the Senate and the House of Representatives, the President has to sign it before it becomes a law. Gagi gets to go to a meeting with the President when he signs the bill, and sometimes she gets to keep the pen he used.

Gagi and the other Senators serve on
committees to learn about and solve important issues in our country.
Each committee holds meetings, called hearings, where the Senators
invite Americans to tell their stories and offer their ideas for solving
America's problems. Then they try to find ways to solve the problems.
Some of Gagi's committees try to stop youth violence and make our
court system better.

★

Committee hearings are often held in
big beautiful rooms like this Judiciary
committee room. The people sitting behind
the microphones are telling the Senators
their opinions about important issues.

Gagi became a United States Senator in 1992.

To become a Senator she had to campaign in California. This meant that she had to travel around the state, meet with constituents, and talk about how she wanted to help them.

   She also had to listen to them tell her about what kinds of problems they had and what kinds of things needed to get done in California. When she was campaigning, Gagi gave a lot of speeches and ate a lot of meals with her constituents. She got to know some of them pretty well.

Gagi talks to people all over California about gun control. She once saw a man get shot and believes that Americans should have fewer guns.

I got to help Gagi campaign, even though I was only a little baby. I was in some ads that ran on television.

At the end of the campaign there was an election. All the citizens of California got to vote on who they thought would make the best Senator.

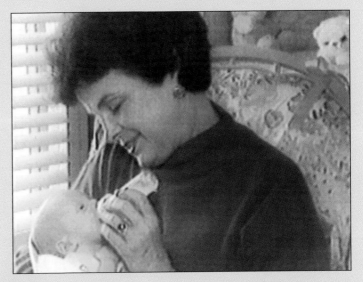

If I had been old enough to talk in this ad, I would have asked everyone to vote for my grandmother because she was the best!

Gagi won! It was pretty exciting. We had a big party the night she was elected, and lots of people came.

★

All the signs say "Dianne" because Gagi likes it when people call her by her first name. But only her grandchildren can call her "Gagi."

17

The only bad thing

about Gagi's election was that Gagi had to move to Washington, D.C., which is all the way across the country. I miss her because she lives so far away, but she comes home a lot when the Senate is in recess—that's what they call it when the Senate goes on a break. I also get to visit her in Washington sometimes. I even go to her office! I like to sit in her chair and pretend that I am a Senator.

Senators keep their jobs for six years at a time. Gagi likes her job and wants to be elected for another term, so I guess she won't be living back at home for a while.

Between the first time I sat in Gagi's office chair and the last, I grew up a lot!

When we miss each other a lot, Gagi and I e-mail each other. She has pictures of me on her screen saver on her computer, so I know she sees me every day, even though I'm not really there.

★

Gagi loves to use e-mail and modern technology. She's pretty good on the computer, even though there weren't any when she was my age.

19

Before Gagi was a Senator, she was the Mayor of San Francisco for many years. Before that, she was the President of San Francisco's Board of Supervisors, which is a group of people that make the laws for San Francisco. Because she lived in San Francisco all her life and helped govern the city for a long time, she knows the city really well and loves to take me places around town.

One place that Gagi and I really like to go is to Golden Gate Park. Gagi says that most people in San Francisco don't have backyards, so it's important for them to have nice parks. When she was Mayor, she told the city officials to make the parks really beautiful.

Buffalo are fun to look at, but you should never pet one. They are fierce!

Now, on weekends, everyone goes to them. I love to visit the buffalo at Golden Gate Park because my grandfather gave them as a gift to the city. I also really like Stow Lake—a pond in the park—because tons of frogs and turtles live there.

Another place we love to go is Lombard Street.

It's one of the highest places in San Francisco, which has a lot of hills. Looking down can be scary, so I try not to. The road winds all over the place! I like to look out at the city, though, and you can see for miles from up there. It's really beautiful.

★

It's pretty windy when you're high up at the top of Lombard Street.

When we go to

Lombard Street, I also like to wave
at the people on the cable cars.
Lots of people in San Francisco
ride them to get around town.
Gagi says hello to the drivers as
they pass by.

★

**The people on the cable car recognized Gagi,
and she enjoyed saying hello to them.**

23

Gagi and I also spend a lot of time at her house

just doing things together. She is teaching me to play the piano, so I practice a lot. I use the same book of music that my mom used when she was a little girl. Gagi taught her to play, too.

I can already play almost all the songs in this book, but Gagi says that practice makes perfect!

Gagi loves to draw flowers,

and we draw together all the time. We pick flowers from her garden and see if we can make our drawings look like the real thing. We use colored pencils and heavy white paper, and we sign our names on the bottom of the drawings when we are done. Gagi frames the best ones and puts them in her house and office. Sometimes she donates them to raise money for charity or gives them to people as gifts.

Gagi calls her drawings "doodles," but they look a lot better than just doodles to me.

Both of us really like to read.

When I was little, Gagi used to read to me, but now I read books to her! If it's nice outside, we go in the garden and read and look at all the flowers. Usually we have sandwiches and chips for lunch and just hang out. If I'm lucky, Gagi lets me have brownies.

Gagi grows all kinds of flowers in her garden, but the lavender is my favorite.

If I spend the night at Gagi's,

I have my own room. I'm even allowed to jump on the bed in there! If my grandfather is away, Gagi and I watch movies and eat popcorn in her big bed.

Gagi says that I'm growing so tall, I almost hit the ceiling when I jump!

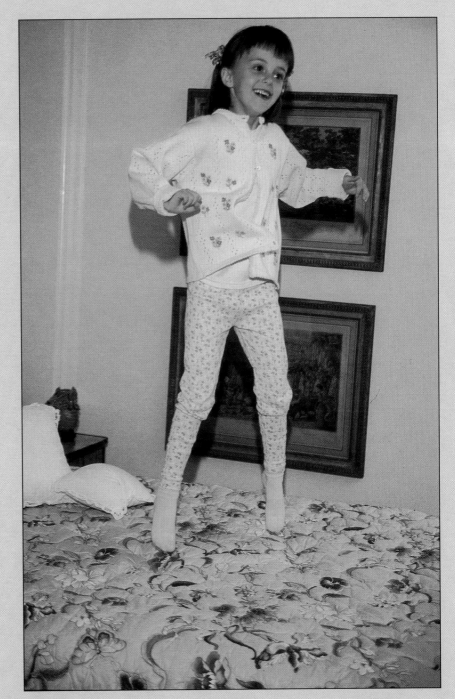

27

Gagi might be a United
States Senator, but she's also
just a cool grandmother.

Everyone tells Gagi, my mom, and me how much alike we look. I don't know if I want to be a Senator like my grandmother, or a lawyer like my mom.

29

When I write her a letter,
I know she'll always answer.

★

If You Want to Be a United States Senator . . .

Work on a campaign. Supporting candidates for office will help you learn about your community, its problems, and the political process.

3 0060 0003129 8

Visit Washington, D.C. Anyone can visit the Senate and watch Senators give speeches on the floor. You can also see speeches on important issues on cable television.

Practice public speaking. As a Senator, you will need to give speeches on the campaign trail as well as on the Senate floor. You may want to participate in the drama or speech clubs at school or give oral reports in class.

Participate in leadership activities. You may want to run for class office, do volunteer work in your community, or start a club at school. All U.S. Senators must be able to lead their staffs and help shape their nation's policy. Dianne Feinstein was Vice President of the student council when she was in college and believes that strong leadership skills are a must.

Find out everything you can about the state you live in. A U.S. Senator represents his or her state to the rest of the world. Learning about your state's natural resources, peoples, attractions, and politics will allow you to show the rest of the country how special your state really is and work to help the people who live there.

Get out and meet people. U.S. Senators must be able to get along with all kinds of people, as they will represent people with different lifestyles and backgrounds. Senators also work with people from all over the world. To be elected, Senators must earn the trust and respect of the majority of their future constituents.

Correspond with your own U.S. Senator. Write to your Senator about issues you think are important, or visit his or her Washington or home office. Senators like to know what their constituents are thinking, as you may find out if you represent your state some day!

Pay close attention in your civics and social studies classes. To be a good Senator you must understand how the U.S. government works. When you are given a chance to do a special project in school, be sure to research information about Congress and the legislative branch.

Learn about social issues. As a Senator, you will need to know about the issues in your community. Getting involved in community activities, such as recycling, literacy programs, crime fighting, and other important programs, will help you understand the needs of your neighbors.